Table of Contents

Contact: Dr. ArchBishop Prophet Shaun Mungroo

P.O. Box 7532 Arlington, Texas 76005

(214) 779-8942

Shaun36@live.com

Acknowledgement

First and foremost I want to give thanks to the Almighty God who has counted me worthy to preach in this end time, and for His grace and divine enabling.

I thank Dr. Brandon Rowe who edited this work.

I will not forget my mentors, fathers (The late Allen Jackson), friends and associates in the ministry: and all those time and space would fail me to mention my spiritual daughters Mittie M. Rollins, Apostle Shay Avery, My Sister Apostle Maria Gbabamosi ,HIOME family (Conshada Mungroo)

I thank God for giving me a good and understanding wife who has always stood by me in times of stress and storms.

God bless my sons and daughters in the ministry whose names are too numerous to mention.

Preface

Prophetic Praying Using Salt' is a 21st century eye opener to the mystery that has been hidden from so many people for over many centuries. It is an indispensable knowledge that every believer and family must have. It is a treasure that guarantees you victory over the satanic forces with which we contend, which diversify and sophisticate their *modus operandi* progressively. And because the knowledge from this book would help you disarm the artillery of the devil, the book would draw the attention of heaven towards you and therefore secure you a special place in the heart of God.

There are a lot of expositions that would be very helpful for the end-time saint, including relevant quotations to buttress every assertion.

The book is a dynamic weapon and an asset to every broad-minded saint who is not parochial in his perception, not quick at passing judgment, but is prepared to study and find out the truth for himself, instead of playing church and throwing aside basic knowledge, simply because his pastor was not privileged to discover it. Knowledge is not static but very dynamic. It is not concealed but readily available to all those who are out to look for it at all cost. The more you seek for, and discover knowledge, the more you realize you really do not know it all. This is an area on which not too many people have written, and so it may appear strange to you. I however advice you to go through the material patiently and objectively, before making your conclusions. This may be the book that may give answers to some of the most difficult questions about your destiny. Daniel said:

Daniel 9:2-3
In the first year of his reign I Daniel understood by books the number of the years, whereof the word of the Lord came to Jeremiah the prophet, that he will accomplish seventy years in the desolations of Jerusalem.
[3] And I set my face unto the Lord God, to seek by prayer and supplications, with fasting, and sackcloth, and ashes:

The knowledge Daniel acquired through books drove him into prayer and fasting for a change in the circumstances around him. This book, doubtlessly, would accord you the privilege of breaking into another realm of spiritual encounter.

Read through the guideline and do not attempt to be ritualistic about it. Know that with or without physical salt, you can still pray the prayer points outlined. There are 60 powerful prayer points to enable you pray well-targeted prayers.

I advise you to own a copy of this book and practice what is written here. Release your faith and share your resultant testimonies with someone. God bless you.

Dr. Anthony Oghenedoro Akoria
(General Superintendent/Founder)
All Faith Revival Church Worldwide,
#4, Miller Close, Off Ogodo Road,
P. O. Box 1827, Sapele, Delta, Nigeria.
September 2004.

SCRIPTURAL BASIS

2 Kings 2:19-22(KJV)

And the men of the city said unto Elisha, Behold, I pray thee, the situation of this city is pleasant, as my lord seeth: but the water is naught, and the ground barren. [20] And he said, Bring me a new cruse, and put salt therein. And they bring it to him. [21] And he went forth unto the spring of the waters, and cast the salt in there, and said, Thus saith the Lord, I have healed these waters; there shall not be from thence any more death or barren land. [22] So the waters were healed unto this day, according to the saying of Elisha which he spake.

2 Kings 2:19-22 (LBV)
Now a delegation of the city officials of Jericho visited Elisha. "We have a problem," they told him. "This city is located in beautiful natural surroundings, as you can see; but the water is bad and causes our women to have miscarriages."
[20] "Well," he said, "bring me a new bowl filled with salt." So they brought it to him.
[21] Then he went out to the city well and threw the salt in and declared, "The Lord has healed these waters. They shall no longer cause death or miscarriage."
[22] And sure enough! The water was purified, just as Elisha had said.

2 Kings 2:19-22(NASB)
Then the men of the city said to Elisha, "Behold now, the situation of this city is pleasant, as my lord sees; but the water is bad, and the land is unfruitful." [20] And he said, "Bring me a new jar, and put salt in it." So they brought it to him. [21] And he went out to the spring of water, and threw salt in it and said, "Thus says the Lord, 'I have purified these waters; there shall not be from there death or unfruitfulness any longer.' " [22] So the waters have been purified to this day, according to the word of Elisha which he spoke.

INNOVATIVE PRAYING

In the last chapter of '*Praying With Power,* C. Peter Wagner wrote on the subject of innovative praying. Here he stressed the need for the body of Christ to engage in creative praying. One of the areas he threw light on is prophetic praying using salt. The following is an extract from the last chapter of the book:

Elisha's Salt

The water in Jericho was bad. Elisha had just received the prophetic mantle from Elijah. Undoubtedly the elders of Jericho had certain doubts about whether Elisha could fill the shoes of Elijah. So they came to him with the problem of the bad water. Elisha sensed that the time had arrived for a public prophetic act. He said, "Bring me a new bowl, and put salt in it" (2 Kings 2:20). When they did, Elisha went to the source of the water and threw the salt into it. He said to the elders, "Thus says the Lord: 'I have healed this water; from it there shall be no more death or barrenness'" (2 Kings 2:21). That is exactly what happened and Jericho's water was fine after that.

Lars-Goran Gustafson of Sweden was living with his family in a large home shared by other Christian families. One morning they turned on the faucet and the water came out dark and had a terrible odor. City officials came to inspect it and condemned the water, shutting off the water main between the well and the house. The families had no idea what to do except to pray and ask God for a solution. That evening two of the residents of the house went to church, and the pastor read 2 Kings 2:19-22. They looked at each other and were amazed to find that each of them, independent of the other, had read exactly the same passage in their devotions that very morning. They concluded they must be hearing from God.

So they gathered the group living in the house, read the 2 Kings Scripture and then asked themselves if they had enough nerve to try to do what Elisha did. It was not easy because this was back in the 1980s when few people were talking about bold prayers and prophetic acts. They prayed and asked each other if they could have faith equal to that of Elisha. One of them said, "Faith is to act on the Word of God and do what it says. So let's go over the passage again. First, the prophet asked for a new bowl."

It so happened that one of the women had just received a gift of two new bowls, so they put salt in one of them, formed a circle around the well house in the backyard, prayed and threw the salt into the well. When they went back to the house, the water came out of the faucet crystal clear. After four days of testing, the puzzled city officials presented a document to them, which said they now had the best water in the community!

Thirty Sacks of Rice

Ravikumar Kurapati, an Indian evangelist, was in trouble. He had gone to a village to plant a new church and one of his first converts was a Hindu farmer. As the season's rice crop grew, the new believer's rice turned out to be the worst in town, full of weeds and wilting plants. He was becoming the butt of jokes and at one point he wondered whether he should have given his life to Jesus. He went to his pastor for prayer. Kurapati encouraged him through the Word of God.

By the next morning, Kurapati had heard from God. He says, "The next day I went with him to his field where almost all the villagers were watching me. I took a bucket of fresh water and prayed. Then I asked the farmer to sprinkle it over his crops." When harvest time came, the amazed farmer reaped no fewer than 30 bags of rice from his field, much more than a plot that size should ever have produced in the best of conditions. The villagers' lives were then opened to the gospel, and a strong church has since been planted.

The preceding two accounts from C. Peter Wagner's book illustrate the amazing results of using common things in faith. This clearly shows that what works for one person in one part of the world also works in another part. The essential thing is for you to release your faith and refuse to be tied to a dogmatic way of approaching the throne of grace. We should not let our dogmatic way of judgment or belief tie down the Holy Spirit in any way. Give the Holy Spirit a chance to direct and lead His church. Stay by your calling and let the Holy Spirit take the lead. The Bible says:

1 Cor. 12:3-7 (KJV)
Wherefore I give you to understand, that no man speaking by the Spirit of God calleth Jesus accursed: and that no man can say that Jesus is the Lord, but by the Holy Ghost. [4] Now there are diversities of gifts, but the same Spirit. [5] And there are differences of administrations, but the same Lord. [6] And there are diversities of operations, but it is the same God which worketh all in all. [7] But the manifestation of the Spirit is given to every man to profit withal.

1 Cor. 12:3-7 (LBV)
But now you are meeting people who claim to speak messages from the Spirit of God. How can you know whether they are really inspired by God or whether they are fakes? Here is the test: no one speaking by the power of the Spirit of God can curse Jesus, and no one can say, "Jesus is Lord," and really mean it, unless the Holy Spirit is helping him.
[4] Now God gives us many kinds of special abilities, but it is the same Holy Spirit who is the source of them all. [5] There are different kinds of service to God, but it is the same Lord we are serving. [6] There are many ways in which God works in our lives, but it is the same God who does the work in and through all of us who are his. [7] The Holy Spirit displays God's power through each of us as a means of helping the entire church.

God expects the church to be creative and innovative, even in prayers, provided it is done in accordance with the will of God and in faith. The testimonies given by C. Peter Wagner above do not contradict the mind and will of God as long as the glory went back to Him. However one needs to be cautious so as not to drift into strange doctrine.

CAUTION

1. This type of prayer should not be seen as one form of occult praying. You must understand that just as in the case of using handkerchief or anointing oil, the power is not in the salt but in the anointing that comes from God as a result of the faith demonstrated.
2. It is possible for the praying saint to pray in faith duly considering and visualizing what the physical salt can do. It is not compulsory that you pray with physical salt, however if you do, you must not idolize it in any form.
3. Do not shift your focus from Jesus to an animate object. He is the Author and Finisher of our faith. Any attempt to shift your focus from Him would make a shipwreck of your faith.

4. You do not need a priest or prophet to be able to pray prophetic prayers. The pre-requisite is for you to be born again, filled with the Spirit and be duly armed with Scriptures.
5. If you must pray with physical salt, you do not need a whole bag of salt to be able to undertake the prayers. Elisha just needed a little quantity of salt in a bowl for the whole land of Jericho to be delivered.
6. Be careful not to fall into the hands of commercial prophets who sell what they call specially consecrated salt. Again, you do not need seven days fast or 'special work' before salt can be consecrated.
7. Do not be instrumental to killing the faith of those who believe in this kind of prayer. Help them to grow and release their faith, instead of quenching their spirits. It may not make sense to you now, but if the Holy Spirit decides to work through what you may see as foolish things, it is all right. Praise God for it.

WHAT IS PROPHETIC PRAYING?

It takes a declaration to organize your destiny. The power of change lies in your tongue. Your tongue is your fighting power, your weapon. As long as you are a believer your fighting power is no more in your hand or in any physical object, but is now resident in your tongue. You get what you say. The Bible says, concerning Jesus:

Rev. 1:16
... out of his mouth went a sharp twoedged sword: and his countenance was as the sun shineth in his strength.

Note that the sword in the Scripture above was not a physical sword, and did not come out of His hand. Rather it came out of His mouth. In essence, whatever word you speak to your enemy would either kill or empower him. It would require your tongue to re-assemble what the enemy has scattered for your own good. Sadly too you can use the same tongue to scatter what God has gathered in your life if not properly used.

God has deposited His power into you. I am talking about the God who calls those things, which be not, as though they were, and declares the end of a thing from the beginning (Rom. 4:17, Isa. 46:10; 48:3). By the working of His power in you, there is the need to exercise this prophetic power before every obstacle mounted by Satan across your way would be surmounted. You must get ready to pray and speak prophetically; get ready to declare or speak the future of a thing the way you expects it to be. Elijah spoke:

1 Kings 17:1
... As the Lord God of Israel liveth, before whom I stand, there shall not be dew nor rain these years, but according to my word.

A prophecy is a supernatural utterance made by God through His anointed vessel to build, edify, comfort and warn His people. It usually comes in an audible, but supernaturally coded voice, to express the mind of God concerning a thing, place, person, or group of persons, or an event.

Prophetic praying, on the other hand, is making prophetic utterances at your prayer altar concerning a thing, whether good or bad, under the anointing and influence of the Holy Spirit.

Prophetic praying is verbalizing or materializing the outcome of an event when it has not taken place. The praying saint sees into the spirit and says what he expects from the event.
Prophetic praying is **addressing inanimate objects as though they have eyes and ears.** It is speaking and commanding spiritual forces to go into action, using the inanimate objects to work. For instance, Prophet Jeremiah spoke to mere sand to reduce a man and his entire generation to nothing.

> ***"O earth, earth, earth! Hear the word of the Lord! The Lord says: Record this man Coniah as childless, for none of his children shall ever sit upon the throne of David or rule in Judah. His life will amount to nothing"***
>
> ***(Jer 22:29,30) LBV***

Can you picture this? It sounds too insane to be true. But it sure happened. It was so soon after the man of God had spoken that the entire generation was hindered by the soil except for Zerubbabel who became a governor, instead of sitting on the throne of David.

Prophetic praying *is choosing a divine order in the Bible and speaking destruction or restoration after that order.* For instance, by picking the event of Pharaoh and his men drowning in the Red sea, the praying saint may say: *Let all my stubborn pursuers, drown and die after the order of the Egyptians at the Red Sea."* There are divine orders and patterns in the Bible that you can programme an event to follow after. For instance, the priesthood of Jesus was after a divine order.

"For He testifieth, Thou art a priest for ever after the order of Melchisedec."

(Heb. 7:17)

You may decide to paralyze, frustrate, destroy, build, prosper or enthrone, yourself or another person or situation, after an existing order. You can equally decide to reject or denounce a particular situation or order and prophesy a change over it.

"... that another priest should rise after the
order of Melchisedec, and not be called
after the order of Aaron?"
(Heb. 7:11b)

In prophetic praying therefore, the praying saint is given the opportunity to call for a new order that would to replace the existing order, as long as it is Scriptural.

"Take off your jeweled crown, the Lord God says, the old order changes. Now the poor are exalted, and the rich brought very low. I will overturn, overturn, overturn the kingdom, so that even the new order that emerges will not succeed until the Man appears who has a right to it.
And I will give it all to him."
(Ezek. 21:26,27) LBV

It would take prophetic praying to usher in a new order in the church, family, community or nation.

Prophetic praying is **demonstrating a very high level of faith and verbalizing our expectation under the leading of the Holy Spirit.** Even though the result may not be immediate, the praying saint should hold tenaciously to his faith and belief in God.

And seeing a fig tree afar off having leaves,
He came, if haply He might find anything thereon: and when He came to it, He found nothing but leaves; for the time of fig was not yet. And Jesus answered and said unto it, No man eat fruit of thee hereafter forever. And His disciples heard it.
And in the morning, as they passed by, they saw the fig tree dried up from the roots. And Peter calling to remembrance saith unto Him, Master, behold the fig tree which thou cursedst is withered away.And Jesus answering saith unto them, Have faith in God."
(Mk. 11:13,14,20-22)

Prophetic praying therefore, is verbalizing our desires in a strong and powerful way to obstacles and mountains and believing strongly that what we have spoken must manifest.

Prophetic praying is **going to the source of the problem and making prophetic utterances to it**. You must first locate the root cause of the problem and then make divine statements that would destroy it. In prophetic praying, you do not shy away from facing reality. Go down to the remote or underground cause of the problem and speak death and destruction to it. When Prophet Elisha was invited to pray for Jericho's water, he went to the spring of the water (II Kgs. 2:19-22). When David faced Goliath, he targeted the unprotected head of the giant. If the cause of the person's problem is an evil background, then prophesy fire into his genealogical foundation; prophesy to his roots, and wipe out the evil foundation, instead of trying to fight the problem from the wrong perspective. Conceivably, it would be out of place to start treating your head when your problem is in the belly or waist region.

Prophetic praying is **prayer backed up by prophetic steps;** for instance, you may decide to walk the dimensions of a particular field or piece of land you desire to buy, making divine utterances and decrees and using anointing oil or salt to seal the decree.

A brother invited me to pray for his block factory, which was more or less draining him financially. When we got there, I saw a heap of blocks mounted at one end of the factory. The Lord led me to the blocks, which, according to the brother were bad and condemned. I went to the heap and addressed it, as if it were a living organism with ears. I spoke to the blocks to go and look for customers to buy them. It may have sounded funny and insane when he heard me talk to the blocks. By the time we left the place, someone came to buy blocks and went straight to the heap of condemned blocks and inquired about them. The manager told him that they were bad, but he insisted he needed them. Whether or not he used them after the purchase does not matter, what mattered was that the blocks obeyed the words of the prophet. Yes, those blocks *went out* to look for someone that would buy them.

I have heard about people who spoke to empty pots of soup to provide food for the family and they obtained good results. Prophetic praying works. You do not need to be a prophet to pray prophetic prayers. You may decide to prophesy against a thing or in favour of it. (Ezek. 11:1-5,13). The most important thing is to prophesy as the Spirit of God leads you.

Prophetic praying is **opening the day with words of prophecy upon which**

the day's business would hang. When you wake up in the morning, make prophetic pronouncements that would order the course of events throughout the day. When you get up, be sure that you start the day by making pronouncements about your spouse, children and all those around you, including the people and customers that you would meet within the day. The preachers should speak good things concerning their members and the sinners in their domain. Prophesy about those you expect to meet and those you would not want to come across. There are certain negative occurrences that happen to people such as unnecessary losses, misunderstanding, accidents, sickness, untimely death, etc, which you do not wish to experience during the day. You need to decree against them through prophetic praying.

Prophetic praying is **activating the ministry of the spoken word**. You should speak anointed words that are capable of arresting situations and simultaneously releasing creative forces. Say what you believe and create a favourable atmosphere for God to work. Words are spiritual ropes that are capable of binding good things together to our advantage, or on the other hand, tying our enemies and problems together for destruction. For instance, creative words can be spoken that can bind up a family that has scattered, or destructive words that can bind enemies and send them to the fire of judgment (Num. 20:8; I Kgs 13:1-5, Jer. 5:14).

WHAT IS SALT?

Chemistry tells us that a salt is the compound formed when all or part of the ionizable hydrogen of an acid is replaced by a metallic or ammonium ions. There are different kinds of salts-soluble and insoluble. From a functional point of view, we can separate two kinds of salts: the well-known edible salt known as common salt, and the industrial salt. By implication, these two are not used for the same purpose. Our main interest here is the common salt chemically known as sodium chloride. Except where otherwise indicated, the term 'salt' in this book refers to this edible salt we use in our every-day cooking.

Salt is a chemical substance that contains sodium and chloride ions as the basic building elements. It is produced by the neutralization reaction of an acid and a base to give this substance sodium chloride ($NaCl$).

Do not be confounded by all the chemical jargons you have just been stumbling over, in case you are not too inclined to chemistry. The fact is that we all know salt. It is available in every household that is used for different purposes. Sometimes, derivatives of iodine are added to salt for nutritional purposes, such as potassium iodide (Encyclopaedia Britannica, 2002):

> *Iodized salt- that is, salt to which small quantities of potassium iodide have been added- is widely used in areas where iodine is lacking from the diet.*
> - *Encyclopædia Britannica, Inc. © 1994-2001*

The word 'salt' thus acquired connotations of high esteem and honour in ancient and modern languages. Examples include the Arab avowal *'There is salt between us'"* the Hebrew expression *'to eat the salt of the palace,'* and the modern Persian phrase *namak haram*, which is literally translated *'untrue to salt'* and means disloyal or ungrateful. In English the term "salt of the earth" describes a person held in high esteem.

The Scripture uses the word salt figuratively. The New Unger's Bible Dictionary quotes:

> *As one of the most essential articles of food, salt symbolized hospitality of the ministry of good men, as opposing the spiritual corruption of sinners (Matthew 5:13); of grace in the heart (Mark 9:50); of wisdom or good sense in speech (Col. 4:6); graceless believers as salt without savor (Matthew 5:13; Mark 9:50); from the belief that salt would, by exposure to the air, lose its virtue; salt pits was a figure of desolation (Zeph. 2:9); "salted with fire" (Mark 9:49) refers to the purification of the good and punishment of sinners.*

Generally speaking, salt is one of the most important substances in human as well as animal diet. Most authorities consider common salt as an essential ingredient of our food. Most people intentionally season their cooking with more or less salt for the sake of palatability. Others depend upon the small quantities, which naturally exist in water and many foods to furnish the necessary amount of salt for the body. Either too much salt or the lack of it creates undesirable disturbance in the animal system. Man and animals alike instinctively seek for this substance to supplement or improve their regular diet. The ancients appreciated the value of salt for seasoning food (Job 6:6). So necessary was it that they dignified it by making it a requisite part of sacrifices (Leviticus 2:13; Ezra 6:9; Ezra 7:22; Ezekiel 43:24; Mark 9:49).

Apart from its nutritional value, salt has other socioeconomic, cultural and religious significance. For instance, it symbolizes hospitality, peace, value, durability, fidelity, purity and cleanliness. In some cultures, to eat salt with someone, whether in the food, or otherwise, is to partake of his hospitality, peace, fidelity and openness or acceptance. This custom of pledging friendship or confirming a compact by eating salted food is still retained among the Arabic people. The Arabic word for "salt" and for a 'compact' or 'treaty' is the same. Once an Arab has received in his tent even his worst enemy, and has eaten salt (food) with him, he is bound to protect his guest as long as he- the guest- remains there.

THE TASTES OF SALT

The taste of salt differs from one type to the other depending on the use and application of it. Some salt taste sour, others taste sweet while the third category taste bitter. Although the salty taste is often associated with water-soluble salts, such compounds (except sodium chloride) have complex tastes such as bitter salt or sour salt. Salts of low molecular weight are predominantly salty, while those of higher molecular weight tend to be bitter. The salts of heavy metals such as mercury have a metallic taste, although some of the salts of lead (especially lead acetate) and beryllium are sweet.

THE IMPORTANCE AND USES OF SALT

> *Salt was used not only as a food, but also as an antiseptic in medicine. Newborn babes were bathed and salted (Ezekiel 16:4), a custom still prevailing. The Arabs of the desert consider it so necessary, that in the absence of salt they bathed their infants in camels' urine.*
>
> *Elisha is said to have healed the waters of Jericho by casting a cruse of salt into the spring (2 Kings 2:20f). Abimelech sowed the ruins of Shechem with salt to prevent a new city from arising in its place (Judges 9:45). Lot's wife turned to a pillar of salt (Genesis 19:26).*
>
> *Salt is emblematic of loyalty and friendship. A person who has once joined in a "salt covenant" with God and then breaks it is fit only to be cast out (compare Matthew 5:13; Mark 9:50). Saltiness typified barrenness (Deut.29: 23; Jeremiah17: 6). James compares the absurdity of the same mouth giving forth blessings and cursing to the impossibility of a fountain yielding both sweet and salt water (James 3:11f).*
>
> *– JAMES A. PATCH*

According to the Encyclopaedia Britannica:

> *Because of its properties as a preservative and seasoning, salt has always been one of the most highly prized mineral resources. Salt is used for processing pickles and cheese and for preserving and curing fish, meat, and some vegetable products. Animal skins and hides are pickled in salt before being processed into leather. It is indispensable in the manufacture of such heavy chemicals as hydrochloric acid, sodium hydroxide (caustic soda), sodium bicarbonate (baking soda), chlorine, and many other*

chemicals. Salt is also used in the manufacture of soap, glaze, and porcelain enamel and is used in metallurgical processes as a flux. When applied to snow or ice, salt lowers the melting point of the mixture. Thus, large amounts are used in northern climates to rid streets of accumulated snow and ice.

- Copyright © 1994-2001 Encyclopædia Britannica, Inc.

At a meeting some young people were discussing the text, "Ye are the salt of the earth." One suggestion after another was made as to the meaning of "salt" in this verse.

"Salt imparts a desirable flavor," said one.

"Salt preserves from decay," another suggested.

Then a Chinese Christian girl spoke out of an experience none of the others had. "Salt creates thirst," she said, and there was a sudden hush in the room. Everyone was thinking: Have I ever made anyone thirsty for the Lord Jesus Christ?

Salt is the commonest thing you can find around. You find it in almost every home. It plays a very important role in our society and can be applied for many uses. In the early days, the Roman Empire adopted salt as money and had to pay her soldiers in salt. They built storage vaults for the salt, which was in the Latin word *salarium*. It is from where the English word, 'salary' was adopted.

> *The economic importance of salt is indicated by the existence, even in the present day, of taxes on salt and of government salt monopolies. In many societies salt has been so highly valued that it has been used for money. The modern English word salary is derived from the Latin salarium, which originally referred to the payments made to Roman soldiers for the purchase of salt.*
> - Copyright © 1994-2001 Encyclopædia Britannica, Inc.

Historically speaking, in some parts of the Western Hemisphere and in India, Europeans introduced the use of salt, but in parts of Central Africa it is still a luxury available only to the rich. Where people live mainly on milk and raw or roasted meat (so that its natural salts are not lost), sodium chloride supplements are unnecessary. Nomads with their flocks of sheep or herds of cattle, for example, never eat salt with their food. On the other hand, people who live mostly on cereal, vegetable, or boiled meat diets require supplements of salt. The habitual use of salt is intimately connected with the advance from nomadic to agricultural life, a step in civilization that profoundly influenced the rituals and cults of almost all ancient nations. The gods were worshiped, as the giver of the kindly fruits of the earth, and salt was usually included in sacrificial offerings consisting wholly or partly of cereal elements.

In early Nigeria and many other African countries, salt served as a medium of exchange for quite sometime. This is so because salt is common, very reliable in the sense that it does not decay, ferment or decompose easily.

Today, man has identified many uses for salt, ranging from household to industrial, chemical, biological and physiological applications. There are also spiritual uses, which is the focus of this book. There is practically no human being that can say that he or she does not need salt for one thing or the other.

Salt, whether common salt or industrial salt, is very important and can be used for the following:

1. The processing of pickles and cheese and for preserving and curing of fish, meat, and some vegetable products. Animal skins and hides are pickled in salt before being processed into leather.

2. It is indispensable in the manufacture of such heavy chemicals as hydrochloric acid, sodium hydroxide (caustic soda), sodium bicarbonate (baking soda), chlorine, and many other chemicals. Salt is also used in the manufacture of soap, glaze, and porcelain enamel and is used in metallurgical processes as a flux. It is also used for the

manufacture of explosives.

3. When applied to snow or ice, salt lowers the melting point of the mixture. Thus, large amounts are used in northern climates to rid streets of accumulated snow and ice.

4. Water-softening equipment uses salt, which exchanges sodium ions for those of calcium and magnesium in the water being treated. Salt therefore is used for the treatment and purification of water.

5. In chemistry salt is used as a conductor of electricity. When in solution or the molten state, most salts are completely dissociated into negatively and positively charged ions and are good electrolytes (conductors of electricity).

6. Salt is used for medication. For instance, where iodine is lacking in someone iodized salt is used as food supplement. Iodine is necessary for the treatment of goitre. Doctors also recommend drip for a patient who is weak and has lost too much water; the drip is made from salt and sugar.

7. Salt is hygroscopic; i.e., under normal conditions, it would absorb water from the atmosphere. Salt dehydrates and lowers temperature. It has been proved scientifically that at 20 °C (68 °F), 100 g (3.5 ounces) of water would dissolve 36 g (1.3 ounces) of salt. The higher the water temperature, the greater the amount of salt that would be dissolved. Dissolving salt in water also would reduce the water's temperature. If 36 g of salt were dissolved in 100 g of water at 15.5 °C (60 F), the resultant solution would lose approximately 3.3-5.5 °C (6-10 °F). Salt melts at 801 °C (1,474 °F) and boils at 1,465 °C (2,669 °F). At 0 °C (32 °F) the specific gravity of salt is 2.165 (i.e., it is 2.165 times as heavy as water).

8. Salt is used for seasoning food. It gives flavour and taste to food. The true taste of food comes out when a reasonable quantity of salt has been introduced (Job 6:6).

9. Salt is used for religious purposes. For instance, in Numbers 18:19, the Jews used it for the ratification of covenants. During the widely televised wedding of Prophetess Bynum Juanita of America, she used salt for the ratification of her marriage covenant. According to her, God replaced the use of shoes with that of salt in ratifying a covenant with Him (Exodus 3:5; Deuteronomy 25:9; Joshua 5:15; Ruth 4:8; 2 Samuel

15:30; Isaiah 20:2;Acts 7:33).

10. It is used for cleansing newborn babies (Ezek. 16:4), rendering a place barren and desolate. It is also useful in the killing of worms.

WHAT IS A COVENANT?

In a general term, a covenant is a usually formal, solemn and binding agreement, or a contract, between two or more people for the purpose of advancing or promoting the course of the parties in the agreement.

> *A covenant is a promise that is sanctioned by an oath. This promise in turn was accompanied by an appeal to a deity or deities to "see" or "watch over" the behaviour of the one who has sworn, and to punish any violation of the covenant by bringing into action the curses stipulated or implied in the swearing of the oath. Legal procedure, on the other hand, may be entirely secular, for law characteristically does not require that each member of the legal community voluntarily swear an oath to obey the law. Further, in ordinary legal procedure the sanctions of the law are carried out by appropriate agencies of the society itself, not by transcendent powers beyond the control of man and society.*

A covenant is a legally binding agreement between two or more people entered into for the mutual benefits of the parties involved. Usually such agreement must spell out the condition(s) under which the parties are liable or obliged to the terms of the agreement. And as long as the parties involved operate within the confines of the agreement a covenant is said to be in existence, but if not, the covenant becomes null and void. Benefits and blessings accrue to both parties involved in a covenant as long as there is faithfulness and commitment to the terms and conditions of the agreement. On the other hand, punishment or penalty is awarded against any party who breaches the terms and conditions of the agreement.

In the Old Testament the Hebrew word *berith* is always thus translated. *Berith* is derived from a root word, which means 'to cut,' and hence a covenant is a 'cutting,' with reference to the cutting or dividing of animals into two parts, and the contracting parties passing between them, in making a covenant (Genesis 15; Jeremiah 34:18-19).

The corresponding word in the New Testament Greek is *diatheke,* which is, however, rendered 'testament' generally in the Authorized Version. It ought to be rendered, just as the word *berith* of the Old Testament, "covenant."

It is expected that a legally binding covenant should be supported by a statement of agreement, an oath by the parties involved, the ratification act, and a higher enforcing organ or power. The statement of agreement is the verbal expression(s) by either party, which defines the extent to which the covenant would go. Usually some covenants go far beyond the contractees to generations yet unborn. For instance, the covenant God had with Abraham was meant to cover future generations (Gen. 17:1-8).

To every covenant there must be an oath sworn to by the parties involved. The oath is an act that enforces the submissiveness of both parties to whatever blessing or judgment that comes out of upholding or breaching the terms of the agreement. In the agreement between God and Abraham we read in Hebrews 6:13,14, of God swearing by Himself to keep His own side I am sure that many of us must have sworn to many covenants before, which we did not keep. Examples are is marriage vow, business vow, and so on.

> *"Again, ye have heard that it hath been said by them of old time, Thou shall not forswear thyself, but shalt perform unto the Lord thine oaths: But I say unto you, swear not at all; neither by heaven; for it is God's throne" Nor by the earth; for it is his footstool: neither by Jerusalem; for it is the city of the great King. Neither shalt thou swear by the head, because thou canst not make one hair white or black. But let your communication be yea, yea; Nay, nay: for whatsoever, is more than these cometh of evil. (Matt. 5:33-37).*

The ratification act of an agreement is the token or action taken by the contractees to seal the agreement. For instance, the agreement between God and Abraham was ratified with the shedding of the blood of animals. The New Testament covenant was sealed with the shedding of the blood of Jesus. Most people seal their agreements with exchange of gifts, sexual intercourse, sacrifices, etc. depending on the nature and type of agreement involved.

Finally, the covenant has to be supervised by a higher power or deity, so that both parties can enjoy the fullest benefits or suffer commensurate penalty in case of fulfillment or breach of the terms and conditions of the agreement. For instance, God and the holy angels entrench godly covenants, while Satan and his cohorts of demons entrench ungodly covenants. When you keep the laws of God no man or demon can stop you from being blessed because God ordains the powers in authority.

> *"Let every soul be subject unto the higher powers. For there is no power but of God: the powers that be are ordained of God. Whosoever*

therefore resisteth the power resisteth the ordinance of **God: and they that resist shall receive to themselves damnation". (Rom. 13:1,2).**

It is better to be under a godly covenant than satanic one. While the former would cover, prosper and protect you, the latter would open doors to demonic attack and harassment.

It is unfortunate that many do not know that every covenant has both the physical and spiritual implications. Marriages, businesses, ceremonies protection and safety covenants, etc, are entered into in the physical but the spiritual side is simultaneously being contracted unknowingly. For instance, when a man disvirgins a girl, the blood that comes out is a seal to the relationship, which becomes a problem when the man refuses to marry the girl. God was not foolish to have made the woman's body like that. Hence, any molestation of virgin becomes an abuse to the spiritual side of the future marriage of the victim. It is even a higher degree of cruelty when mature people rape innocent children. They are not only doing them physical harm but also exposing them to demonic sex manipulations, which later in life turn out to be hidden covenants and problems requiring ministration.

Covenants may be entered into personally; they can be inherited from parents, or, by virtue of religious beliefs, place of work, place of residence and so on. Some covenants may be hidden in dreams, sex, blood, occult and so on. For instance, a man who serves God is in a religious covenant with his Maker, while the one who joins himself to a secret cult is in an occult covenant with demonic powers and with Satan. And, of course, you know that the devil can fix you up anytime he needs a prey, by going into that cage or prison you have sold yourself into by that demonic covenant. A demonic covenant gives the devil legal grounds to operate in the life of the victim; hence these covenants have to be broken (Jer. 2:26-28, 37, 14; 44:25-27). You are not a slave but a freeman.

THE IMPLICATIONS OF A BINDING COVENANT

1. Both parties are committed to fulfilling the terms and conditions of the covenant.

2. It covers the parties involved in the covenant and those who are represented in the covenant.

   Deut. 29:14-15
   Neither with you only do I make this covenant and this oath; [15] But

with him that standeth here with us this day before the Lord our God, and also with him that is not here with us this day:

3. It can change or alter the lives of those involved as they faithfully implement it.

4. It can deliver into your hand what your sweat could not. In other words it can make you acquire what you do not qualify for.

5. It enables you to share from the other party what he has to offer according to the terms of the covenant. In other words a covenant does not end with connection but extends to sharing and communion.

   1 Samuel 18:1-4
   And it came to pass, when he had made an end of speaking unto Saul, that the soul of Jonathan was knit with the soul of David, and Jonathan loved him as his own soul. [2] And Saul took him that day, and will let him go no more home to his father's house. [3] Then Jonathan and David made a covenant, because he loved him as his own soul. [4] And Jonathan stripped himself of the robe that was upon him, and gave it to David, and his garments, even to his sword, and to his bow, and to his girdle.

6. It provides a legal framework by which the parties must operate and whatever benefits are available to the parties are guaranteed.

7. It must not be broken without the consent of both parties. If that is done it attracts a penalty or a curse that brings judgment upon the one guilty of the breach offence. 2 Samuel 21:1-6; Jeremiah 34:8-22; Ezekiel 17:13-19

Based on an ancient custom, covenants were not only concluded with an oath (Genesis 26:28; Genesis 31:53; Joshua 9:15; 2 Kings 11:4). Rather, they were confirmed by slaughtering and cutting an animal into two halves between which the parties passed, to indicate that if either of them broke the covenant he would be as the slain and divided beast (Genesis 15:9-10, 17-18; Jeremiah 34:18-20). Moreover, the covenanting parties often partook of a common meal (Genesis 26:30; Genesis 31:54; cf. 2 Samuel 3:20 with 2 Samuel 3:12), or at least of some grains of salt.

From Biblical records covenants were ratified by:

* By giving the hand. Ezra 10:19; Lam. 5:6;

Ezek 17:18

* By loosing the shoe. Ruth 4:7-11
* Written and sealed. Neh. 9:38; Jere. 32:10-12
* By giving presents. Gen.21:27-30; 1 Sam.18:3-4
* By making a feast. Gen. 26:30
* By a monument. Gen. 31:45-46; Gen. 31:49-53
* By offering a sacrifice. Gen.15:9-17; Jere.34:18-19
* By oath.
* By salting. Lev. 2:13; Num. 18:19; 2 Chron. 13:5

Hebrews 6:16-17

For men verily swear by the greater: and an oath for confirmation is to them an end of all strife. [17] Wherein God, willing more abundantly to shew unto the heirs of promise the immutability of his counsel, confirmed it by an oath:

THE MYSTERY OF THE SALT COVENANT

Salt is emblematic of loyalty and friendship. In the Old Testament times, a person who had undergone or joined in a 'salt covenant' with God and then broke it was only fit to be cast out (compare Matthew 5:13; Mark 9:50).

One of the major uses of salt as highlighted above is for religious services. Salt is used to ratify and seal covenant with God. The priests offered salt along with sacrifices whenever they appeared before God on behalf of the people.

According to the New Unger Bible Dictionary:

> *Not only did the Hebrews make general use of salt in the food both of man (Job 6:6) and beast (Isaiah 30:24), they also used it in their religious services as an accompaniment to the various offerings presented on the altar (Leviticus 2:13, "every grain offering of yours, moreover, you shall season with salt"). The salt of the sacrifice is called "the salt of the covenant of your God," because in common life salt was the symbol of a covenant. The meaning that salt (with its power to strengthen food and preserve it from putrefaction and corruption) imparted to the sacrifice was the unbending truthfulness of that self-surrender to the Lord embodied in the sacrifice, by which all impurity and hypocrisy were repelled. In addition to the uses of salt already specified, the inferior sorts were applied as manure to the soil or to hasten the decomposition of dung (Matthew 5:13; Luke 14:35). Too large a mixture, however, was held to produce sterility; and hence also arose the custom of sowing with salt the foundations of a destroyed city (Judges 9:45), as a token of its irretrievable ruin.*

The Bible records fifteen great covenants, amongst which is the salt covenant. These covenants are:

1. ***The Solaric Covenant-*** The covenant of eternal season of fruitfulness as long as the solar system continues (Gen. 1:14-18; 8:22; Psa. 89:34-37; Jer. 31:35-37; 33:19-26).

2. ***The Edenic Covenant-*** The covenant made with man before the fall of Adam in the Garden of Eden. It was a conditional covenant based on their obedience (Gen. 1:26-3:24).

3. ***The Adamic Covenant-*** The covenant made with Adam and Eve after their fall, which ushered in the Dispensation of Conscience (Gen. 3:14-19; Rom. 5:12-21).

4. ***The Cainic Covenant-*** The pledge made by God to Cain of vengeance on anyone who dared killing him (Gen. 4:11-15).

5. ***The Noahic Covenant-*** The covenant that ushered in the Dispensation of Human Government after the flood where God detailed man to rule, enjoy a curse-free earth, fruitfulness, eat animals as meat but not the blood and sealed the covenant by rainbow (Gen. 8:20-9:26).

6. ***The Abrahamic Covenant-*** The covenant that ushered in the Dispensation of Promise after God confused the tongues of men and stayed them from building the Tower of Babel. God promised to make of Abraham a great nation, to bless him, to bless those who blessed him and to curse those who cursed him (Gen. 12:1-3; 13:14-18; 15:1-21; 22:15-18; 26:1-5). The circumcision of all male children ratified the covenant.

7. ***The Hagaric Covenant-*** The covenant made with Hagar to multiply her seed, Ishmael, and make him a great nation on the face of the earth (Gen. 16:7-14; 17:20; 25:12-18).

8. ***The Sarahic Covenant-*** The covenant of fruitfulness with Sarah in her old age. Her name was to change from Sarai to Sarah, her child was to continue the Abrahamic covenant and she was to be the mother of many nations (Gen. 17:15-19; 18:9-15).

9. ***The Healing Covenant-*** This covenant was made for Israel and to those who are the descendants of Abraham by faith. It is for those who would diligently seek God. It guarantees healing for all. (Exod. 15:26; 23:25; Lev. 26:14,15).

10. ***The Mosaic Covenant-*** This is also known as the Old Testament or Old Covenant (Exod. 20:1-24; 2Cor. 3:6-18).

11. ***The Levitic Covenant-*** The covenant of peace, blessings and everlasting priesthood to the house of Levi as a result of the good deed of Phinehas for turning away the anger of God through his zeal (Num. 25:1-14).

12. ***The Palestinian Covenant-*** The covenant with the nation of Israel characterized by scattering them, repentance, restoration, national conversion, judgment of their oppressors and national prosperity (Lev. 26; Deut. 11:8-32; 27: -30:20; Zech. 12:10-14; 14; Isa. 11:1-12; Rom. 11).

13. ***The Salt Covenant-*** The covenant made with Israel concerning the sacrifices they were to offer forever (Lev. 2:13; Num. 18:19; 2Chron. 13:5;

Ezek. 43:22,24).

14. ***The Davidic Covenant-*** This covenant was made with David and his house through the Prophet Nathan and was conditioned upon obedience (2Sam. 7:1-17).

15. ***The New Covenant-*** This is the covenant initiated by Christ that cuts across the 27 books of the New Testament. It came into effect by the shedding of the blood of Jesus. However, Jesus did not come to abolish the laws but to fulfill them (Matt. 26:28; 2Cor. 3:6-18; Heb. 8:6).

Biblical salt covenant is an everlasting covenant, which God's children must enter into with their God. Every believer is supposed to be a 'spiritual salt' offered at the altar of the community for men and women to taste from, so that they can make peace with God (Matt 5:13; MK 9:50).

In Palestine and its environment, salt is used in provoking peace between people who are enemies. Once salt is offered and two archenemies eat from it, they are automatically bound together in a covenant relationship forever. Salt has a spiritually unifying force to those who have faith in the salt covenant. In the book of Leviticus 2:13; the Bible says:

> ***"And every oblation of thy meat offering shalt thou season with salt; neither shalt thou suffer the salt of the covenant of thy God to be lacking from thy meat offering: with all thine offerings thou shalt offer salt."***
>
> ***(Lev. 2:13)***

As a symbol of friendship God required the Jews to offer salt along with their meat offering. By such offering He (God) is welcome to partake in the spiritual table prepared by them. There could be a meat offering offered at the table but the covenant salt must not be lacking. It was the salt of the covenant that made the covenant package complete. God expected the Jews to welcome Him as a friend to come and dine with them. He too has a table prepared for His children. (Ps 23:5), but He must first be invited to our tables before inviting us into His (Rev. 3:20). We must be ready to make peace with God before He would make other things be at peace with us (Job 22:21-25, Prov. 16:7). The offering of the salt of covenant in all their offerings is what secures peace for them. It was never to be missing from their tables. The priests must offer salt whenever they were offering sacrifices on behalf of God's people.

> ***"When thou has made an end of cleansing it, thou shalt offer a young bullock without blemish, and a ram out of the flock without blemish. And thou shalt offer them before the Lord, and the priests shall cast salt upon them, and they shall offer them for a burnt offering unto the***

Lord."

(Ezek 43:22,24)

King Artaxerxes, commanded that whatsoever Ezra the priest wanted for the house of God be released to him. He ordered that one hundred talents of silver be released to him, including an hundred measures of wheat, an hundred baths of wine, an hundred baths of oil, and salt without prescribing how much (Ezra 7:20-23). Why? It was simply because he understood the fact that the priest was required by God to always make salt available in all his offerings.

The Jews laid up salt in a portion of the temple known as the salt chamber. It was from here that salt was served periodically by the priest to season offerings meant for the Lord. God got into a covenant of salt with Aaron and his descendents by giving to him all the heave offerings (i.e. whatever is taken out and kept from the offerings) and all dedicated and consecrated things of the Israelites. They were to be his own by reason of the anointing upon his life as a priest. The Amplified Version of the Bible reads:

> ***"And the Lord said unto Aaron, And I, behold, I have given to you the charge of My heave offerings (whatever is taken out and kept of the offerings made to Me), all the dedicated and consecrated things of the Israelites; to you have I given them (as your portion) and to your sons as a continual allowance forever by reason of your anointing as priests."***
> ***(Numb. 18:8) The Amplified Bible***

By what covenant were they given? It was by a covenant of salt. Read verse 19:

> ***"All the heave offerings (the lifted-out and kept portions of the holy things which the Israelites give to the Lord I give to your sons and your daughters with you, as a continual debt forever. It is a covenant of salt (that cannot be dissolved or violated) forever before the Lord for you (Aaron) and your posterity with you."***
>
> ***(Numb 18:19) The Amplified Bible***

Aaron and his descendents were not to have inheritance in the land of Israel but to make the Lord God their own portion and inheritance. Being a direct employee of God. Aaron and his descendents were provided for from the altar of the Lord. He was to eat and live comfortably from the divine provision from God. God's employees never lack, they are well catered for by Him. However, there must be a covenant of salt to seal or secure this divine provision forever.

At the battlefield between Abijah the King of Judah, and King Jeroboam, the former- Abijah- invoked the covenant of salt, which David got into with God to overthrow the latter. King Jeroboam came to the battlefield with 800,000 soldiers against the 400,000 soldiers of Abijah. Unmoved by the twice as many numbers of soldiers of Jeroboam he declared:

> ***"Ought ye not to know that the Lord God of Israel gave the Kingdom over Israel to David for ever, even to him and to his sons by a covenant of salt?"***
>
> ***(II Chron 13:5)***

By this, Abijah was reminding Jeroboam of the covenant of salt David had with God concerning Judah, and warning him of the consequences of his action. But Jeroboam, with his obsessed heart, would not heed to the warning.

2 Chron. 13:12-19

And, behold, God himself is with us for our captain, and his priests with sounding trumpets to cry alarm against you. O children of Israel, fight ye not against the Lord God of your fathers; for ye shall not prosper.
[13] But Jeroboam caused an ambushment to come about behind them: so they were before Judah, and the ambushment was behind them. [14] And when Judah looked back, behold, the battle was before and behind: and they cried unto the Lord, and the priests sounded with the trumpets. [15] Then the men of Judah gave a shout: and as the men of Judah shouted, it came to pass, that God smote Jeroboam and all Israel before Abijah and Judah. [16] And the children of Israel fled before Judah: and God delivered them into their hand. [17] And Abijah and his people slew them with a great slaughter: so there fell down slain of Israel five hundred thousand chosen men. [18] Thus the children of Israel were brought under at that time, and the children of Judah prevailed, because they relied upon the Lord God of their fathers. [19] And Abijah pursued after Jeroboam, and took cities from him, Bethel with the towns thereof, and Jeshanah with the towns thereof, and Ephrain with the towns thereof.

The outcome of the war was that Jeroboam lost 500, 000 of his soldiers and Abijah lost none. Jeroboam did not recover after this war because he had out stepped his bounds. He had tangled with the wrong man- a man under a covenant- and in fact, God had to kill him. Abijah on his own part waxed great and enjoyed the seat that David had salted. The Bible says:

2 Chron. 13:20-21

Neither did Jeroboam recover strength again in the days of Abijah: and the

Lord struck him, and he died.
[21] But Abijah waxed mighty, and married fourteen wives, and begat twenty and two sons, and sixteen daughters.

No one could overthrow king David all his days in spite of the numerous enemies that were around him, both within and without. God was tied to His covenant, which was ratified by salt. May God do the same with you today in Jesus name.

King David, in his days, always offered sacrifice to his God and offered salt along with it. This covenant of salt became a preservative to his throne and a defence in the time of war. Even though Jeroboam took part of the kingdom in the time of Rehoboam, yet he could not keep it. His generation and himself were soon cut off because he turned to idolatry (I Kgs 14:9-11) and he violated the salt covenant. The kingdom still went back to the house of David.
Encapsulated in God's covenant with David, were seven distinct blessings viz:

1. God promised to secure his life and that of his children forever (II Sam. 7:13-16).
2. God promised to establish his throne forever (II Sam. 7:12-16).
3. God promised to remove bitterness from his life and introduce sweetness instead (II Sam. 7:12-19).
4. God promised him deliverance and protection from the forces of wickedness (Ps 89:20-23, II Sam 7:10).
5. God promised him Fatherly care forever. You can imagine the protection and coverage a mortal man can enjoy in having God as his Father (II Sam. 7:14).
6. God promised him a covenant of eternity (II Sam. 7:10-16).
7. God promised him that He would preserve him from being afflicted by the nations of the world. By implication, He was not to be defeated and swallowed up by other nations (II Sam. 7:14).

> ***"And the fame of David went out into all lands; and the Lord brought the fear of him upon all nations."***
> ***(I Chron. 14:17)***

How lovely would it be to see yourself entering into the same covenant pact with the God of David? Make yourself available to God by a covenant of salt today and you would see that none of His promises would fail, just as He kept His word towards David and Israel (I Kgs 5:3-5, 8:56).

Summarily, the salt covenant is a perpetual covenant that brings man and God, man and his circumstances or opposers, at peace. By it, God would make your enemies to be at peace with you since your life pleases Him (Heb 11:6; Prov. 16:7).

God expects the believer's life and speech to be seasoned with salt (Mk 9:49,50; Col 4:6). Once this is done, He can present you to the world for use in seasoning, preserving, healing, edifying and delivering those in need. This was why Jesus referred to the believer as the salt of the world.

> ***"Ye are the salt of the earth: but if the salt have lost his savour, wherewith shall it be salted? It is thenceforth good for nothing, but to be cast out and to be trodden under foot of men."***
>
> ***(Matt. 5:13)***

May you not lose your saltiness. May men not tread you down. May you be the salt that is empowered by God and proudly displayed for the world to benefit from. But do you know that you cannot do so without first surrendering your life to Jesus? Of course, it is true. I counsel you to ask Jesus to come into your life right away before you can proceed to the next stage. God bless you as you do.

WHY DID GOD CHOOSE TO USE SALT AS A COVENANT PACK?

1. It may be because salt does not decay.

2. It may be because salt is not perishable.

3. It may be because salt is common and can be found everywhere.

4. It may be because salt cannot be destroyed by fire.

5. It may be because of its purifying nature.

6. It may be because of the two wonders of salt and water.

> *Salt is a wonder. Salt is composed of two poisonous substances. How is it possible that salt, which is necessary to life, is composed of sodium and chlorine, either of which if taken individually, would kill you?*
> *Water is a wonder. Its chemical formula is H_2O. That means it has two parts of hydrogen for each part of oxygen. Oxygen is flammable; hydrogen readily burns. Unite hydrogen and oxygen into water and you put out fires with it!*

God is a God of wonders and He loves to use things that are wonderful.

7. It may be because it is a symbol of eternity that cannot be corrupted or destroyed.

> *It is still not uncommon to put salt into a coffin, and we are told the reason: Satan hates salt, because it is the symbol of incorruption and immortality.*
> *– Papatus*

THE MYSTERY OF THE DEAD SEA AND SALT

Research has revealed that the concentration of salt in the Dead Sea is ten times higher than the second most salty sea or lake in the world. Indeed the Dead Sea is very salty. Every liter of its seawater contains an average of 30 grams of salt and other minerals. It is one of the greatest sources of salt in the world.

No animal or plant can exist here. Only a few species of fish are found in it, although it is not true that birds, which get close to its vapour, fall down dead.

However, because of its high specific gravity, no one would ever sink or drown while bathing there. Nobody has ever committed suicide there by drowning. It was said that Vespasian, commander of the Roman legion, which later destroyed Jerusalem in AD 70, heard of this fact. He tested it by ordering slaves to be thrown into the sea waves with their hands and feet tied. To prove these claims, the slaves floated.

The wealth in the Dead Sea is so enormous as to be almost unbelievable. All the manufactured goods, fruits and vegetables exported from Israel are nothing in comparison with the mineral wealth in that Sea.

After General Allenby captured Jerusalem in 1917, a British geologist began to investigate the mineral riches of the Dead Sea. The outcome about this investigation was breath taking! Its tremendous reserve is estimated at 22 thousand million tons of magnesium chloride, 12 thousand million tons of common salt, 6 thousand million tons of calcium chloride, two thousand million tons of potassium chloride, and one thousand million tons of magnesium bromide. The economic value of these chemicals would come out to the staggering figure of $1,270,000,000,000. This amount would be equal to the combined wealth of the United States, Great Britain, France, Germany and Italy.

The knowledge of the above information can help you to pray prophetically.

For instance a man who renders his life as a *Dead Sea* to the enemy would have succeeded in:

1. **Rendering his life a death trap and danger zone for spiritual oppressors.**
2. **Rendering his life unpalatable to eaters of flesh and suckers of blood (Psa. 27:2).**
3. **Barricading his life from wicked arrows.**
4. **Making his life a reservoir of riches and wealth.**
5. **Forcing whatever virtue enemies have buried out of his reach to stay afloat like the axe head that floated in 2Kgs. 6:6.**

CAN A MAN BE SALTED?

Mark 9:49-50
For every one shall be salted with fire, and every sacrifice shall be salted with salt. [50] Salt is good: but if the salt have lost his saltness, wherewith will ye season it? Have salt in yourselves, and have peace one with another.

According to Adam Clarke, the Scripture above generally supposes that our Lord means, that as salt preserves the flesh- with which it is connected- from corruption, so would the everlasting fire of hell. This inconsumable fire would have the property of not only assimilating all things cast into it, but of making them inconsumable like it. In other words, just as this fire cannot be quenched, so would anything, and in fact, anyone, thrown into it remain incombustible and intact, even though he may suffer intense pain from its heat.

Salt and fire are purifiers. They have the capability of removing dross from unclean things and making them good for use. ***"For every one,"*** the Bible says, ***"shall be salted with fire, and every sacrifice shall be salted with salt."***

A look at the books of Numbers 31: 23, 1Corinthians 3:13-15 and Romans 12:1 would drive the message home. The Bible says:

Numbers 31:23
Every thing that may abide the fire, ye shall make it go through the fire, and it shall be clean: nevertheless it shall be purified with the water of separation: and all that abideth not the fire ye shall make go through the water.

1 Cor. 3:13-15
Every man's work shall be made manifest: for the day shall declare it, because

it shall be revealed by fire; and the fire shall try every man's work of what sort it is. [14] If any man's work abide which he hath built thereupon, he shall receive a reward. [15] If any man's work shall be burned, he shall suffer loss: but he himself shall be saved; yet so as by fire.

Romans 12:1
I beseech you therefore, brethren, by the mercies of God, that ye present your bodies a living sacrifice, holy, acceptable unto God, which is your reasonable service.

We are living sacrifices unto God and the works we are doing in the house of God shall be tested by fire on the last day. For your life to defy corruption and be preserved before God it has to be salted, not necessarily with physical salt. Trapp, in his notes wrote:

> *"The Spirit, as salt, must dry up those bad humours in us which breed the never-dying worm; and, as fire, must waste our corruptions, which else would carry us on to the unquenchable fire."*

The fire of the word and Spirit of God must try every one of us and make us fit and qualified for heaven. When you allow the word and the Spirit try you, you become an offering or a living sacrifice unto the Lord as in the book of Romans 12:1 above. You become the type of offering that Isaiah 66: 20,22 refers to.

Isaiah 66:20
And they shall bring all your brethren for an offering unto the Lord out of all nations upon horses, and in chariots, and in litters, and upon mules, and upon swift beasts, to my holy mountain Jerusalem, saith the Lord, as the children of Israel bring an offering in a clean vessel into the house of the Lord.

Isaiah 66:22
For as the new heavens and the new earth, which I will make, shall remain before me, saith the Lord, so shall your seed and your name remain.

My prayer for you is that it would be well with your soul and that you would be a pleasing and incorruptible sacrifice unto the Lord on the last day. May you not be among the abhorring lot of verse 24 of the preceding Bible passage.

Isaiah 66:24
And they shall go forth, and look upon the carcases of the men that have transgressed against me: for their worm shall not die, neither shall their fire be quenched; and they shall be an abhorring unto all flesh.

These are the group of people who are salted with the fire of hell, as eternal victims of divine justice. We must of necessity be sacrificed to God, after one way or other, in eternity; and we have now the choice of either the unquenchable fire of his justice, or of the everlasting flame of His love. Ensure that ye have, at all times, the preserving principle of divine grace in your hearts, and give that proof of it, which would satisfy your own minds, and convince or silence the world. Live in brotherly kindness and peace with each other: thus shall all men see that you are free from ambition, (see Mark 9:34), and that you are the disciple of Jesus indeed. It is possible for the salt to lose its savor, and yet retain its appearance in the most perfect manner (Matthew 5:13).

According to Bible Background Commentary on Mark 9:50, *Jesus apparently changes salt to a positive metaphor, perhaps meaning "peace." That real salt (as opposed to the impure salt mixtures available from some inland sea deposits) by definition does not lose its saltiness only reinforces the strength of the image.*

With these facts in mind a man who prays prophetic prayer using salt is indirectly rendering his life pure, incorruptible, refined, reserved, untouchable, preserved and useful unto the Lord. The salt spiritually changes your smell and you become a sweet aroma or flavour unto God. Read more about how to change your smell in my book, ***'The Result Is Out!'***

SALT COVENANT IN ACTION

Numbers 18:19
All the heave offerings of the holy things, which the children of Israel offer unto the Lord, have I given thee, and thy sons and thy daughters with thee, by a statute for ever: it is a covenant of salt for ever before the Lord unto thee and to thy seed with thee.

The Bible Commentary of Adam Clarke on Numbers 18:19 reads:

> ***It is a covenant of salt***—*That is, an incorruptible, everlasting covenant. As salt was added to different kinds of viands, not only to give them a relish, but also to preserve them from putrefaction and decay, it became the emblem of incorruptibility and permanence. Hence, a covenant of salt signified an everlasting covenant. We have already seen that, among the Asiatics, eating together was deemed a bond of perpetual friendship; and as salt was a common article in all their repasts, it may be in reference to this circumstance that a perpetual covenant is termed a covenant of salt; because the parties ate together of the sacrifice offered on*

the occasion, and the whole transaction was considered as a league of endless friendship.

There is no one who goes into a spiritual salt covenant with God that does not enjoy divine benefits. The ones I have seen pray or sign up a salt covenant with God have recorded one outstanding testimony or the other. *Many have released their faith and salted peace into their lives, salted evil out of their lives, salted favour into their lives, paralyzed the wicked arrows of darkness fired at them, disgraced the spirit of death, salted closed doors open by fire and rendered their lives a dry place to Satan.*

When God wanted to wipe out the land of Sodom He salted it by fire. The Bible says:
Deut. 29:23 (NASB)
'All its land is brimstone and salt, a burning waste, unsown and unproductive, and no grass grows in it, like the overthrow of Sodom and Gomorrah, Admah and Zeboiim, which the Lord overthrew in His anger and in His wrath.'

Deut. 29:23 (LBV)
They will see that the whole land is alkali and salt, a burned over wasteland, unsown, without crops, without a shred of vegetation--just like Sodom and Gomorrah and Admah and Zeboiim, destroyed by the Lord in his anger.

My prayer for you is that you would obtain victory and breakthrough as the Lord seals His covenant of healing, deliverance, prosperity and eternity with you by salt.

Recently a member of my church who attended one of our salt covenant services took the salt we blessed to the village where her mother, who had stroke and paralysis, was receiving treatment in the shrine of an idol priest. She prayed and salted her paralyzed mother and the stroke and paralysis disappeared instantly. The lady walked on her feet, all by herself, from the shrine back home. When the native doctor saw what happened he became angry and accused the sister of using a greater fetish power.

A lady who was having problems with delivery had undergone labour for over a week. While she was in that condition a deaconess from our church was invited to minister to her. She ministered with the covenant salt, and the God of heaven intervened. She was delivered of her baby without further stress. You can imagine the relief the woman, the concerned doctors and nurses, and other patients around had after this great deliverance.

This same deaconess was invited to minister to a dead baby. She also decreed life into that baby using the covenant salt and the dead baby was restored to life. God will always back up His word.

There was another sister in our church who had a chronic abdominal pain associated with her menstrual cycle. According to her, sometimes when the pain came, she would roll on the floor and the husband, who happened to be a pastor, would pray all the prayers he could, yet there were no results. One day, the husband was out on an official duty and the pain came calling. She took salt, decreed, made a solution of it and drank. Thereafter, she had a nagging pressure to go to the toilet. In the toilet a black worm came out of her and that was the end of the problem.

Another sister, after one of our salt covenant meetings, salted her almost outdated Mercedes car and decreed for a new car. A few days later the husband surprised her with a new V-boot Mercedes car. The husband was not aware of the prophetic steps his wife took days earlier.

A brother recently narrated the following gruesome experience. "In my dream I saw a mouse moving close to me. To my greatest surprise this mouse metamorphosed into a human being. All of a sudden, I saw a knife in 'his' hand. 'He' then raised up the knife and, in a flash, gave me a stab in the abdomen. When I woke up I began having very excruciating pains where I had been stabbed and this pain persisted for a quite sometime. But during one of the salt programmes we had, I applied the covenant salt to that part of the body, prayed, and made prophetic utterances. Guess what? That was the last time I ever experienced that pain. Praise God"

In the same meeting there was a sister invited by her friend. It was her first time of attending the programme. She had an abdominal problem for which she needed to see the doctor. She then got into a salt covenant relationship with God. On the third day of the programme, she fell under the anointing in the course of the prayers and a word of knowledge came from the man of God saying that the Lord was about to heal someone with chronic abdominal pain. By the time she got up, the Great Healer, Jesus, had already perfected her healing. Thank God she got into that salt covenant with God.

Some months earlier, the husband to our sister, the man who bought the Mercedes for his wife, was denied his well-deserved promotion in the office. Surprisingly all his colleagues were promoted. As you would expect, he came home dejected. The wife then remembered she had some covenant salt at home, and that God had a covenant of perpetual peace with her family. She therefore decreed by faith with the salt. A week later when he returned to the office, his immediate boss apologized, saying that they discovered there was a mistake on his promotion issue, and the situation was going to be rectified immediately. Within the same week, his promotion letter was given to him, a situation that had never taken place in the history of that company. Usually once promotions were over, any omitted person would have to wait till the next promotion exercise, even if was going to take ten years. He was told by his bosses and colleagues that the God he was serving was great- to have been able to make management revisit his issue,- and that he should never stop serving this God. Because of this breakthrough, people now had confidence in God and started regarding him as a very spiritual man. He was immediately made the leader of the company's fellowship. This is how God can express His power through salt.

You can bring your family, church, business, community and nation under a salt covenant relationship and enjoy peace. You can pray and salt evil out of your home and wherever you are.

A lady noticed that for fifteen years her husband had been dating a strange woman and had refused sleeping on the same bed with her, let alone making love to her. She phoned me from a distant place and I explained the salt covenant to her, with enough Scriptures and prayer points to pray. She prayed and salted the family home and chased strange spirits from her bedroom. When the husband returned it was a different story. For the first time in fifteen years he felt remorse and apologized for mistreating her in the preceding fifteen years. She called back a week later to appreciate the goodness and faithfulness of God to His eternal covenant of salt. Today there is peace in that home.

There was also a couple that was leaving together in peace and harmony in a city. For simplicity, let us call the wife Samantha. One day, Samantha's mother-in-law came into the house with a demonic substance prepared from salt. An idol priest had given this substance to her. She emptied the content in the house. In the process of spreading the demonic salt she made some incantations. Unknown to her, the house help saw her do this. The consequences of this old woman's action followed immediately. The man stopped eating food prepared by his wife. This went on for quite sometime until the house help told Samantha what her mother-in-law had done. When she discovered this she also took salt, blessed it, decreed on it, and carried out a cleansing process in the home. She prayed prophetic prayers to reverse the effect of the demonic salt and to counter the demonic decrees made by her mother-in-law. Thank God it worked. Peace was restored in Samantha's home thereafter. Until the rod of Moses turned into a serpent it could not swallow the serpents of the Egyptians.

God recruited the following armies to fight for Moses against Pharaoh:

1. From Ashes (Exod 9:8,10).

Exodus 9:8,10
And the Lord said unto Moses and unto Aaron, Take to you handfuls of ashes of the furnace, and let Moses sprinkle it toward the heaven in the sight of Pharaoh.

And they took ashes of the furnace, and stood before Pharaoh; and Moses sprinkled it up toward heaven; and it became a boil breaking forth with blains upon man, and upon beast.

2. From the Dust (Exod 8:16,17)

Exodus 8:16-17
And the Lord said unto Moses, Say unto Aaron, Stretch out thy rod, and smite the dust of the land, that it may become lice throughout all the land of Egypt. [17] And they did so; for Aaron stretched out his hand with his rod, and smote the dust of the earth, and it became lice in man, and in beast; all the dust of the land became lice throughout all the land of Egypt.

3. From the Water (Exod 7:19-20)-Blood and (Exod 8:5-6)-Frogs
4. From the Heavens (Exod 9:22,23)- Hail
5. From the Wind (Exod 10:13-15)- Locusts
6. From Nature (Exod 10:21-23)- Darkness
7. Through Evil Angels (Exod 11:4-8)-Angel of death

God still works wonders today for His children. He can fight battles for us. One of the most effective ways is when we pray prophetic prayers using salt. Attacking the power source of your problems with salt can bring down mountains and obstacles.

A lady could not sleep well in her home. She noticed that there was this spirit husband that was always molesting her sexually anytime she got on her bed. It was a Jericho-like problem to her because inspite of all the deliverances she had undergone, there was no breakthrough. One day, after we consecrated salt for her, she took a step of faith and prayed prophetic prayers using salt. She anointed her bedroom by salt and prayed violently. That was the end of the strange visitor. She could, thereafter, sleep well.

A final year student of the University of Benin (Nigeria) was attacked with stroke (one side of the body was paralyzed). She refused to allow the devil get away with it and quickly applied the salt we prayed over to the spot of paralysis and cried violently against the spirit of paralysis. The Lord delivered her instantly and she came to share her testimony to the humiliation of Satan. A young man who was bewitched and touched with a charm, cried to one of my pastors that organ had disappeared. Thank God for the covenant salt. He salted that part of the body and it was restored. Charms and diabolical materials cannot withstand the power of God released through salt.

One sister in my church discovered that cataract grew in one of her eyes, which, from medical advice, could only be removed by surgery. She traveled with her husband to see the specialist. The moment she got to the door of the clinic, she heard a voice reminding her of the salt that I prayed over. There and then, she told the husband that they must return home. This almost annoyed the husband, but being a spirit-filled man he agreed and co-operated with her. They got home and applied the covenant salt, calling on the God of Akoria (the author). God honoured their faith and she was healed. What an amazing power of covenant salt. It is not only an instrument of peace but also releases healing anointing.

There was a particular lady who had been experiencing serious oppression from territorial forces. After the first salt covenant service we held in our church, she was, at night, led to pray prophetic prayers and anoint the well in her compound with salt. The moment she dropped the salt into the well, hell broke loose. She started hearing a roaring sound from the well. The fighting continued as the water was rising and pouring everywhere in a fountain-like fashion. The following morning they saw a very big dead python, with its head resting on the mouth of the well and the rest of the body still inside the well. What killed this mysterious beast? It was the power of God released through covenant salt. The power of God disgraced the power of the territorial python that had, for years, held the people in that area captive.

One day, the spirit of death woke me up from my sleep about midnight. The spirit was prepared to kill that night. By the unction of God, I took my covenant salt and entered into prophetic praying. I salted the house and made prophetic utterances and the spirit of death left.

So far, there have been about five dead or dying people who have received their lives back when we applied the covenant salt and prayed prophetic prayers. One of them died and was laid upon the church altar. The prayer warriors salted him and left him there. God in His power brought him back to life by respecting the covenant pact of salt we have with Him.

The Bible says:

> *"For every one shall be salted with fire and every sacrifice shall be salted with salt."*
>
> *(MK 9:49)*

Have you salted your life with the fire of God? Has your family ever been salted? What about your home, money and office? Take a step of faith and salt the situation that has refused to let you go. You must salt that land of yours that has been a source of worry and conflict for you.

THE SALT ACRONYMN:

S	=	**Seals and Seasons you**
A	=	**Anchors and Approves you**
L	=	**Liberates and Looses you**
T	=	**Tunes and Turns your captivity around**

After Abimelech overthrew Shechem, he buried salt in the soil. Why? This was in order to render the land barren and desolate (Judges 9:45). By reason of salt, it is possible to render every unproductive area of your life dead. In other words, it is possible to revive the productivity of every dead part of your life. It is also possible to render your life a favourable place for the Holy Spirit, and a dry and desolate place to the devil. As long as salt can kill vegetation and worms, whatever the enemy sows in the garden of your life has to die.

A boss planned to sack a Christian sister who was innocent of the alleged crime. She was led to pray and reverse the wicked plan of the oppressor after the order of Mordecai and Haman. She prayed at home that night and in the morning she salted her office as she had been instructed in her dream. Before long, her boss was sacked in her place. Salt can waste an evil plot and waste life spiritually. The Bible says:

> *"The whole land will be burning waste of salt and sulphur - nothing planted, nothing sprouting, no vegetation growing on it. It will be like the destruction of Sodom and Gomorrah, Admah and Zeboiim, which the Lord overthrew in fierce anger."*
>
> *(Deut. 29:23) NIV*

> *"He will be like a bush in wastelands; he would not see prosperity when it comes; He will dwell in the parched places of the desert, in a salt land where not one lives."*
>
> *(Jer 17: 6) NIV*

Once a place is spiritually declared a salt pit or salt land, whatever the enemy sows or plants in that place cannot grow. The land, life, place or thing that is rendered perpetually desolate to Satan by salt cannot be destroyed or manipulated by him. (Zeph 2:9; Ezek 47; II Sam 8:13,14). Every earthworm enemies working against your life and victory must be salted to death. Whatever has burrowed into the soil of your life must die just like the earthworm. Sickness in your body can also be salted to death. This is not the time to pamper or feed your problems. Whatever must die must do so today (Zech. 11:9)

The Bible says that a spiritual man is *mad* and the prophet is a *fool* (Hosea 9:7). I am sure you know the Scriptures are using these two words 'mad' and 'fool' in an opposite sense. The spiritual man may do what looks foolish; or may, himself, look mad to those who are not spiritual. But it is in doing these that he obtains astounding results from God. Most of the time it takes spiritual madness to get God to intervene in our situations.

The meticulous and know-it-all Christians do not always receive miracles from God, as the following story clearly illustrates.

After learning about what the Lord did in one of our salt covenant services, a sister from Roman Catholic Church decided she would attend the next service. She came with her salt. By the time we were through she left with the salt she had come with. The next day, she travelled to another city to visit someone in the hospital. When she got there, she saw that the patient- a pregnant woman- could not deliver on her own. She was to be operated upon to bring the baby out. At this juncture, she prayed and gave the salt to the lady. As soon as she took the salt she got into immediate labour and delivered safely. Thank God the Roman Catholic lady released her faith at what looked like the foolishness of a prophet. This may look really funny and absurd to the skeptics.

There was also the case of a lady whose husband had been flirting all around with all kinds of strange girls. According to this lady, the man had never done her good thing for years. The Spirit of God led her to salt his food and make prophetic pronouncements. She did this and guess what followed? The man abandoned those strange ladies and started doing her favour as if he were a charmed man. She was able to salt those other women that soul-tied her husband out of his life.

I visited a couple in Europe and had a salt covenant prayer with the family. While we were praying, the power of God came mightily and the woman who was seriously under witchcraft affliction suddenly burst into tears as the power hit her. She fell on the chair and had a wonderful time with the Holy

Spirit, praising, worshipping and laughing hysterically. Meanwhile we continued with our prophetic decrees and salt covenant prayers. By the time we were through, the witchcraft plantation in her abdomen and legs had disappeared. God fulfilled His part of the covenant and came down to unlock His daughter. The operation she was scheduled for the following week was taken care of by God while she was under power. God disgraced Satan by this covenant of salt.

You can salt favour into your life. In the same vein, you can salt evil out of your life. It is all a matter of your faith and confidence in God. If you believe in II Kings 2:19-22 and ignore the voice of critics, you will obtain your breakthrough by salt. But remember; do not cross the borderline into occultism. Lift up Jesus in everything you do. 2 Kings 2:19-22 says:

And the men of the city said unto Elisha, Behold, I pray thee, the situation of this city is pleasant, as my lord seeth: but the water is nought, and the ground barren. And he said, Bring me a new cruse, and put salt therein. And they brought it to him. And he went forth unto the spring of the waters, and cast the salt in there, and said, Thus saith the LORD, I have healed these waters; there shall not be from thence any more death or barren land. So the waters were healed unto this day, according to the saying of Elisha which he spake.

PROPHETIC PRAYING USING SALT

2 Samuel 8:13
And David gat him a name when he returned from smiting of the Syrians in the valley of salt, being eighteen thousand men.

2 Kings 14:7
He slew of Edom in the valley of salt ten thousand, and took Selah by war, and called the name of it Joktheel unto this day.

1 Chron. 18:12
Moreover Abishai the son of Zeruiah slew of the Edomites in the valley of salt eighteen thousand.

2 Chron. 25:11
And Amaziah strengthened himself, and led forth his people, and went to the valley of salt, and smote of the children of Seir ten thousand.

Zeph. 2:9
Therefore as I live, saith the Lord of hosts, the God of Israel, Surely Moab shall be as Sodom, and the children of Ammon as Gomorrah, even the breeding of nettles, and salt pits, and a perpetual desolation: the residue of my people shall spoil them, and the remnant of my people shall possess them.

2 Kings 2:19-22
And the men of the city said unto Elisha, Behold, I pray thee, the situation of this city is pleasant, as my lord seeth: but the water is naught, and the ground barren. [20] And he said, Bring me a new cruse, and put salt therein. And they bring it to him. [21] And he went forth unto the spring of the waters, and cast the salt in there, and said, Thus saith the Lord, I have healed these waters; there shall not be from thence any more death or barren land. [22] So the waters were healed unto this day, according to the saying of Elisha which he spake.

You are never defeated on the ground of your covenant. From the Scriptures above the children of God won all the battles fought in the valley of salt. When a man has made peace with God by a salt covenant he receives all the backing he needs to win every battle of life confronting him. The book of Job says:

Job 22:21-30
Acquaint now thyself with him, and be at peace: thereby good shall come unto thee. [22] Receive, I pray thee, the law from his mouth, and lay up his words in thine heart. [23] If thou return to the Almighty, thou shalt be built up, thou shalt put away iniquity far from thy tabernacles. [24] Then shalt

thou lay up gold as dust, and the gold of Ophir as the stones of the brooks. [25] Yea, the Almighty shall be thy defence, and thou shalt have plenty of silver. [26] For then shalt thou have thy delight in the Almighty, and shalt lift up thy face unto God. [27] Thou shalt make thy prayer unto him, and he shall hear thee, and thou shalt pay thy vows. [28] Thou shalt also decree a thing, and it shall be established unto thee: and the light shall shine upon thy ways. [29] When men are cast down, then thou shalt say, There is lifting up; and he shall save the humble person. [30] He shall deliver the island of the innocent: and it is delivered by the pureness of thine hands.

The covenant of salt would first reconcile you with God and earn you a place in heaven before it would benefit you. God is not in a hurry to turn you into an overnight millionaire He is rather in a hurry to get you into your proper place in His kingdom where you are secure, before overthrowing your mountains. If you have settled your salvation with God then you are qualified to take necessary steps to pray prophetic prayers using salt.

Settling the issue of your salvation gets the salt inside you rather than outside. In other words a man that has given his life to Christ is, spiritually speaking, automatically transformed into salt to do more than what physical salt would do. You need the salt in you more than you need it from the shop. It makes you more loaded and more ready to operate anytime, anywhere.
The Bible says:

Matthew 5:13
***Ye are the salt of the earth:** but if the salt have lost his savour, wherewith shall it be salted? it is thenceforth good for nothing, but to be cast out, and to be trodden under foot of men.**

Another Scripture says that we should have the salt in us:

Mark 9:50
Salt is good: but if the salt have lost his saltness, wherewith will ye season it? Have salt in yourselves, and have peace one with another.

Do you have salt in you? Have you made peace with God? If your answer is in the affirmative then you are ready to pray prophetic prayer using salt. But if not, then just go on your knees and confess your sins and ask Jesus to come into your life.

Having read through the book to this point, you have, no doubt, acquired the required knowledge concerning the workings of salt, both spiritually and physically. It is not enough to acquire the knowledge. You must apply it. This is what is known as wisdom. To pray prophetically, therefore, you must go through the knowledge you have acquired concerning the properties, uses and importance of salt and apply them to your situation one by one. For instance,

1. **<u>SALT IS A PRESERVATIVE</u>**
   (II CHRON.13: 5)

There are many things in your life that you may want God to preserve from decaying. Examples include your marriage, family, life, ministry, business, job, name, the anointing, position and relationship with people and so on.

All you need to do is focus your mind on God (with or without physical salt in your hand), then decree and prophesy into that department of your life. Say what you are saying with boldness and confidence and believe it will happen, as you want it. For instance, you may say:

> "My position in this company shall be preserved after the order of the throne of Jesus. I salt my position and decree that no power can move me out, in the name of Jesus."

2. **<u>SALT GIVES FLAVOUR. IT SEASONS OR SWEETENS. IT GIVES OR BRINGS OUT THE TASTE OF FOOD</u>** (Job 6:6, Lev. 2:13, Mk. 9:49)

There are so many people who have things to offer in the open market of life but no man is ever asking them what they have. There are a lot of talents that are wasting away. There are so many people that have reached the age of marriage and yet no one is asking their hand in marriage. All these are the result of the Satan's activities.

The believer needs to ask God to salt his life, certificates, wares, church hall, etc, and ask for divine favour or patronage. Whatever is making people not to develop interest in you, or in whatever you are doing for a living, should be salted for favour to manifest. Those who do not attract favour before their spouses, employers, helpers or neighbours must ask God to season their lives so that their stories would change for the better.

You must not forget to season your relationship with God. There has to be a free flow of good things from God into your life; and you must occupy a special place in the heart of God so that your request would receive speedy answers. Once the Spirit of God makes His way into the life of a mortal man God never hides His face from him (Ezek. 39:29). Getting into a salt covenant with God *tries you* and *makes* you a suitable vessel for God to dwell in you and use you.

3. **SALT PURIFIES AND CLEANSES (EZEK 16:4)**

There are a lot of spiritual impurities that make people, places or things unacceptable, unattractive and repugnant to people. This dross may be curses (inherited, hidden or personal), evil covenants, satanic marks and spiritual coding, sin, bloodguilt and all kinds of pollution you can think of.

God expects you to be cleansed from this spiritual dross and be at peace with Him. Salt is a purifier (Mk. 9:49,50). You can pray prophetically and ask Him for spiritual cleansing through the salt. Ask God to cleanse you and make you covenant-worthy.

Pray that whatever spiritual dross has been attached to your life be completely removed by salt. Any strange spirit defying the temple of your life must be wiped out. You must carry out a spiritual sanitation of your life, wares, dwelling place, *et alia*.

Indeed, it is time to decree spiritual cleansing into your life, your home, property, etc. Any spiritual power operating in your home and preventing you from enjoying what God has for you must be wiped out by salt. Carry out a spiritual sanitation of your environment by salting everywhere by fire. You must salt the peace of God into your life, home, finance and every department of your life, right away.

4. **SALT DEHYDRATES.**

It removes water from one level of concentration to another level of concentration by a scientific process called osmosis.

When you remove water from an organism, the organism would dry up and die immediately. You may apply this principle in the sense that when you salt any problem, you are squeezing life out of that problem, and so it must die. Therefore you can also pray by retrieving every good thing forces and agents of darkness have sucked from you spiritually through the process of spiritual osmosis. Render every problem spot in your life dry. Command your problem to shrink in size until it dries up. It may not make sense to the natural man but it will certainly work for the spiritual man.

5. **SALT CAN BE USED TO MANUFACTURE EXPLOSIVES, AND IS CAPABLE OF KNOCKING AN ENGINE.**

Prophetically, you can visualize the source of your problems as coming from an engine and visualize salt being poured into that engine in the spiritual realm. Pray intensively with this picture on the canvass of your imagination until you see the engine explode and become completely destroyed.

If you want to go an extra mile, you may decide to salt any evil personality manufacturing or multiplying problems against you to death. It is better to deal with the root of a problem than deal with the shoot.

6. **SALT CAN KILL AND RENDER DESOLATE** (Judges 9:45, Ezek.47: 9,11, Jer. 17:6; Deut. 29:23, Zeph. 2:9).

There are a lot of things and evil personalities that must die before you can have your peace. It is up to you to salt them to death. Sickness must die out of your body, and so it needs salting. What about poverty and hardship? What about witchcraft forces? Well, it is up to you to sort out what qualifies to be destroyed or to die in your life.

If you decide to pray prophetically by burying salt as Abimelech did in Judges 9:45, it is up to you, provided your faith can carry you until you see the results.

Judges 9:45
And Abimelech fought against the city all that day; and he took the city, and slew the people that was therein, and beat down the city, and sowed it with salt.

Using salt, you can render your life, family, finances, dwelling place, marriage, property or ministry a dry and too desolate place to the devil. You may even declare that any trespasser receives the judgment of God. Thereafter whatever happens to them would be between them and God.

Salt can kill vegetation or trees. You may also wish to apply salt to any evil tree growing in the foundation of your life. The trees of witchcraft, failure, poverty, disappointments, hatred, curses, rejection, non-achievement, bitterness, sin, bad habits, sorrow, and whatever you consider evil in your life; as well your family, ministry or business, can all be salted to death.

Has it ever occurred to you why God decided to punish the covetous wife of Lot by turning her to a pillar of salt? Well, think of it and add that to your prophetic prayer points.
Do you know that the name given to the Dead Sea came as a result of the degree of salinity of the water? Because of the enormity of its salinity any living thing that goes into it dies. This is another way you can render your life a desolate place to evil arrows and bullets fired at you by the devil. Make sure that your body becomes a dry place to satanic arrows. The Bible says that no weapons fashioned against you by your enemies shall prosper (Isa. 54:17).

7. **SALT CAN BE USED FOR MEDICATION. IT BRING HEALING AND CURE** (II Kgs. 2:19-22)

The land of Jericho was suffering from the curse earlier placed upon it by Joshua. This was why the water caused barrenness and unproductivity. The land was healed after Prophet Elisha poured in salt and made prophetic utterances. Jericho's situation changed forever. It is my prayer that you would experience the same thing as we approach the end of this book.

A sister who had believed God for a child came to our church to look for her sister. Coincidentally, it was during one of our salt covenant services. She wanted to leave after seeing her sister but the Chief Shepherd (Jesus) who led her there constrained her to stay. According to her, the service became more and more interesting as people came up to say their testimonies of the previous salt covenant services during which God met their needs. To cut the story short, she was given part of the blessed salt, which she took home and used as the Lord led her. That night, she received a divine visitation and God personally carried out a surgical operation upon her. The worm eating up her womb was divinely killed. That month she missed her period, and this, by implication, meant she was pregnant. She also sowed her battle seed. Today, she is a mother of a child. (See Chapter Six of my book, ***"I Can Never Be Poor In Life"*** for a discourse on battle seed).

In that same service, there was a man who read my book, ***"Acid And Machine Gun Prayers"***, and had traveled in from London to Nigeria. Previously, this man was greatly rich, but had now become pauper under mysterious circumstances. This happened when the government froze his accounts and confiscated his assets. This man prayed violently in that meeting and went home with the salt. By the time he got home he salted his house and made prophetic pronouncements. Two weeks later, when I met him in Lagos, he testified to the fact that after applying the salt a mysterious insect that had been making a screeching sound in his house for years came out of its hole and died in the open. In that same week, the government released his frozen accounts and assets after many years. To God be the glory and praise.

God can heal anything if you can allow Him access into that *no-go* zone of your life. If you can cast away doubt, pride and sin out of your life and yield unto Him, He would extend His covenant of peace and perpetuity into your life.

The level of faith with which you pray prophetic prayers would determine the results that would follow. Whether or not you use physical salt should be a matter between you and your God. Do not be ruffled about what people may say; they neither know what you are going through, nor its intensity. Depend on your spirit and pray your prayers. I have never seen someone who was punished by God for taking a step of faith, and you would not be the first in Jesus name.

8. <u>SALT CAN BE USED TO GET RID OF SNOW AND ICE FROM THE STREETS</u>

Whatever represents snow or ice in your life, and constitutes a nuisance to the journey of your life has to be challenged and salted by fire. Everything that is reducing your spiritual temperature must clear out by salt and fire. Pray that the Holy Spirit organizes a street-to-street cleansing of your destiny and make your everyday journey a fruitful and enterprising one.

9. <u>SALT CONDUCTS ELECTRICITY.</u>

Your life needs to be wired and connected to the divine source of power. When you are disconnected you would suffer spiritual power failure and blackout. Once you notice that your life is no more generating the desired voltage to get you going, you must pray and salt yourself by fire. Ask God to get you connected back to the power source and release a fresh anointing into your life.

May your life give out the required degree of voltage and fire that would help you survive as a believer and help others under you to also survive.

10. SALT CAN SEAL AND RATIFY A RELIGIOUS COVENANT

Salt and make yourself covenant-worthy. You must be a partaker of the divine blessings of God. But how can this be? It is by salting yourself by the blood and fire of God.

King David understood this and therefore salted his throne. This had the effect of making him a covenant child of God. There lay the secret of his victory and special influence with God. He ruled the kingdom on a permanent basis making way for his Seed, Jesus, to rule forever and ever.

2 Chron. 13:5(KJV)
Ought ye not to know that the Lord God of Israel gave the kingdom over Israel to David forever, even to him and to his sons by a covenant of salt?

2 Chron. 13:5 (NLT)
Don't you realize that the Lord, the God of Israel, made an unbreakable covenant with David, giving him and his descendants the throne of Israel forever?

2 Chron. 13:5 (GW)

Don't you know that the Lord God of Israel gave the kingdom of Israel to David and his descendants forever in a permanent promise?

Let us conclude with this story. A lady- let us call her Sandy- got married to a man. Unknown to her, the mother-in-law was not happy about it. One day, the mother-in-law came to visit at the time Sandy's husband was still in the office. She came with demonic salt in her hand, which she got from a witch doctor. To Sandy's surprise the countenance of the mother-in-law changed towards her. Just as a judge would pass a death sentence on a helpless accused person, she authoritatively gave Sandy a seven-day ultimatum from that day, during which she must get all her belongings and leave the house. Then she spat on the salt and spread it all over the house, which instantly disappeared before Sandy's eyes. Shortly after she left the house, Sandy's husband came back home from the office and refused to say a word to her. She stood there surprised, scanning through her mind what could have gone wrong. She remembered they did not have any misunderstanding before he left home for the office in the morning. When Sandy tried asking him questions, it only made matters worse. She then tried using words to pet him but he retorted, "Shut up!" She tried again and fighting started. Right from that day on, peace deserted the home. What was it that drove peace away? The demonic salt! The painful thing was that her friends were now advising her to visit witch doctors instead of inviting the Prince of peace to take over. I wished she understood the salt covenant; that would have reversed the effects of the demonic salt.

As we pray prophetically, I remind you again that you are the salt of the world. Jesus has spiritually placed you on the public table of the world so that people can taste of you to preserve, sweeten, heal, enjoy, purify and cleanse their lives, families, community, and your nation. We cannot afford to disappoint Jesus, since, wherever we go, we are representatives of the kingdom of God. May God see and interpret your tears. Amen.

GUIDELINES IN PRAYING PROPHETIC PRAYERS USING SALT

1. Confess your sins and make peace with God. Be sure that you are sincere to God and to yourself.

2. Get rid of doubt and unbelief you have ever had concerning praying with salt, especially now that you have seen it written in black and white in the Bible. Do not do a thing because somebody told you. Rather do it after you have read the Bible and have been convinced.

3. Ask God to anoint you to pray prophetically and well-targeted prayers.

4. Take a bowl and put salt inside it as Elisha did in II Kgs 2:19-22. If you feel you can do without physical salt, go ahead. Let your faith carry you.

5. Begin to minister the salt to the source or root of your problem as Elisha did for Jericho. Deal with the deities in charge of your problem as you mention and salt them to destruction.
   Expel every one of them and minister salt to their strongholds in the land, sea and heaven.
   If you are doing land liberation, go to locations where their shrines are located and deposit salt there as you accompany it with prophetic pronouncements. Do what you are led to do under the guidance of the Holy Spirit and by the counsel and assistance of an experienced deliverance minister.

6. Take with you words and Scriptures that would help you pray well-targeted prayers. Use your Scriptures to contest your legal rights that the enemy has infringed upon. Verbalize your claims and resist the devil, by the fire of the word (Jer. 5:14).
   For example, you may decide to read through chapters of Ps. 35:1-9, 26-28 as you walk, pray and salt every verse into manifestation in your life. Pray prayers that are relevant but guided by the Scripture you have selected.

7. Seal your prayers and worship God from the depth of your soul. Sing songs of gratitude and appreciation to your Father in heaven.

   For instance, a song like this.

   We are grateful, O Lord (Halleluyah)
   We are grateful, O Lord

For all you have done for us (Halleluyah)
We are grateful, O Lord

PRAYER POINTS

1. *Confession, repentance, renunciation and reconciliation.*

2. Every unprofitable department of my life, be seasoned by salt.

3. Every stubborn tree growing in the foundation of my life! I minister salt and fire to your roots, in the name of Jesus.

4. O Lord, terminate whoever is trying to terminate my life, by salt and fire.

5. Whatever is militating against my victory in life, be wiped out by salt and fire.

6. I enter into a covenant of salt with God and I cancel suffering from the agenda of my life.

7. Anything in me that is not glorifying God in my life, be salted to death.

8. I salt divine favour and excellence into my life.

9. Any evil personality raising satanic salt altar against my life and breakthrough, die.

10. Any enemy of progress that qualify for the title of spiritual earthworm and is digging into the foundation of my life, be salted to death.

11. Any power delaying the manifestation of good things in my life, I wipe you out by salt.

12. You my confiscated good things lying idle in satanic warehouse, I salt you to manifestation.

13. O Lord, salt my life and baptize me with tear-drying miracles.

14. I salt every department of my life and I walk into dumbfounding

miracles.

15. Any evil pot containing my goodness in the spirit realm, explode and let go of it, by salt.

16. Holy Spirit, anoint and salt my eyes to locate my divine riches.

17. Any anti-miracle force delegated to withstand me, I salt you to death by fire.

18. Holy Spirit, salt me and usher me into a feast of miracles.

19. I challenge the power source of my unrepentant enemies by salt and fire.

20. You salt of the Almighty! Convert the well of poverty in my life into the well of prosperity.

21. Anything in me magnetizing evil into my life, be salted by fire.

22 You enemies of progress delegated to pull me down I pursue and overtake you by salt and fire.

23. Any river of curses and covenants flowing into my life and family, receive salt and dry up.

24. Any sickness and poison surviving in my blood system, I salt you to death.

25. Any demon attached to my body, I overthrow you by the salt of the Almighty.

26. I apply the salt of the covenant to any evil soul tie working against me. Evil soul tie! Break now.

27. I salt myself from minimum to maximum.

28. Iron-like cases and problems! Break by the salt of the covenant.

29. You ruling deities troubling this land, I expel you by salt and fire.

30. You household wickedness! I stand against you with the salt and fire.

31. O Lord, salt my way to breakthrough.

32. Any moving object in my body, I salt you to death.

33. Every member of my family! I pass you through salt and fire.

34. Any thing I have lost through dream, I salt you back into my life.

35. Any evil participant in my dreams, I salt you by fire.

36. You evil messenger delegated to frustrate my effort in life, I salt you and your message to death.

37. Evil messages of death and hell prepared for me, expire by salt and fire.

38. O Lord, make me covenant-worthy by salt and fire.

39. My covenant with God is unbreakable. My life shall advertise perpetual peace through the covenant of salt.

40. Through the covenant of salt, I possess my possession.

41. You witchcraft spirits, sitting upon my divine riches and wealth, I overthrow you by salt and fire.

42. Any good thing that familiar spirits have buried far away from me, manifest by salt and fire.

43. By the salt of the covenant! O Lord, speak prosperity (healing, deliverance, promotion, favour, joy, power, peace, restoration, freshness) into my life .

44. By the salt of the covenant! You my departed riches walk back into my life now.

45. By the salt of the covenant! O Lord, multiply your signs and wonders in my life, now.

46. I bury salt against every stubborn case causing me unrest and I render my life as a desolate place to the demons.

47. By the salt of the covenant! I prophesy a change into my life for good.

48. By the salt of the covenant! I refuse to suffer what my ancestors have suffered.

49. By the salt of the covenant! I prophesy to my life, "No man can kill me before my time."

50. O God of Abraham! Usher me into greater wealth through the covenant of salt.

51. God of Hezekiah! Interpret my tears because of the covenant of salt.

52. Anything that is missing in my spirit, soul and body, be replaced now, by salt and fire.

53. Thou salt of the covenant. Minister life, power and strength into every tissue of my body.

54. O Lord, season my life and make me profitable to you and to my generation.

By the covenant of salt, I break every covenant I have consciously and unconsciously signed with the devil.

(Now hold some salt in your hand and pray the following prayer points)

56. With this salt I am holding in my hand, I carry out a spiritual cleansing of my home, finances, property, position and family.

57. With this salt I am holding in my hand, I reverse any evil done by enemies to my destiny.

58. With this salt I am holding in my hand, I make peace with God and

speak peace into every department of my life.

59. With this salt I am holding in my hand, I make it impossible for my life to be emptied.

60. With this salt I am holding in my hand, my eagle shall fly and land in my Canaan.

www.ingramcontent.com/pod-product-compliance
Ingram Content Group UK Ltd.
Pitfield, Milton Keynes, MK11 3LW, UK
UKHW051135260726
13967UKWH00010B/3064

9 781105 634284